STANLEY STREET REA

Mee-Lee from Number 3

written by Mandy Ross

illustrated by Sami Sweeten

Birmingham Advisory & Support Service
BASS

Birmingham City Council
Education Service

Mee-Mee Lee from Number 3 liked to keep fit.

"It keeps my heart happy," she said.

tennis
football
running

"Let's have a Stanley Street Keep-Fit Fun Day today," said Mee-Mee one morning.

"But first, let's feel our hearts beating slowly."

watch
heart
ba-doum, ba-doum

The Keep-Fit Fun Day started at Daisy Plum's at Number 1. Daisy said, "We can have a potato and spoon race."

First they dug up the potatoes.

pant
potato patch
dig here
puff
pile of potatoes
spade

Then, when everyone was ready, Mee-Mee said,

"Potato Racers! On your marks, get set, GO!"

potato off spoon
oops!

finish

feeling warm
pant
puff

Next, Hotwheels Hugh at Number 2 said, “Let’s have a wheely whizz!”

When everyone was ready, Mee-Mee said,

"Wheely Whizzers! On your marks, get set, WHIZZ!"

Lively Clive from Number 5 said,
"Let's have a jive!"

When everyone was ready, Mee-Mee said,

"Lively Jivers! On your marks, get set, JIVE!"

very warm
zooty-toot-toot
lively jiving
bit sweaty
puff
pant
pink cheeks
bit sweaty

Next, Trixie Rix at Number 6 said,

“Let’s fix up an under-and-over race.”

Everyone helped to fix up the race.

old blanket
string
bits of wood
post

Then, when everyone was ready, Hotwheels Hugh said,

"Under-and-Over Racers! On your marks, get set, GO!"

start
puff
under here
round here
sweaty
pinker cheeks
along here

Next, the Lately-Thwaites from Number 8 said, “Let’s have a piggy-back race.”

Everyone found a piggy or a back.

Then, when everyone was ready,
Mee-Mee said,

"Piggy-Back Racers! On your marks,
get set, GO!"

piggy-back-Trixie
puff
very sweaty
piggy-back Clive
piggy-back-teddy
piggy-back-baby
pant
very hot
red cheeks

At the end of the last race, Mee-Mee said, “Let’s feel our heart beats again.”

All the happy hearts were beating quickly now, *pitter-patter, pitter-patter, pitter-patter!*

"It's fun to keep fit!" said Mee-Mee Lee from Number 3.

Published by Birmingham Advisory Support Service
Balden Road, Harborne, Birmingham B32 2EH

ISBN 1-898244-80-4
Project Co-ordinator: Fran Stevens
Editor: Lorraine Horsley
Designer: Anne Matthews

Three Counties Aero Engineering BCAR AMR/106	01256 381330
Thurston Avionics Ltd BCAR DAI/9064/86 E2 JAR CAA.00188 A1-A3.C2.C3.C5.C6.C13	01708 688341/4
Thurston Helicopters (Engineering) Ltd JAR CAA.00002 A3.C8.C10.C11	01737 823514
TNT Aircraft Maintenance Services JAR CAA.00098 A1.B1	01279 66666
Trenchard Ltd BCAR AMR/234 M3	01846 651749
Truman Aviation Ltd BCAR AMR/393 M3	0115 9815050
Ultraflight Microlights Limited **T/A Spectrum Aircraft** BCAR DAI/8958/85 A1(Microlight)	01283 791917
Vectis Aviation Services BCAR AMR/328 M3	01983 405520
Vintage Engine Technology Ltd JAR CAA.00026 B2	01767 651794
Westair Engineering Services Ltd JAR CAA.00060 A2.A3.C5.C6.C8.C14.C16	01253 404925
Westley Aircraft BCAR AMR/248 M3	01234 751807
Westwards Airways (Lands End) Ltd JAR CAA.00016 A2	01736 788601
White Waltham Airfield Ltd JAR CAA.00394 A2	01628 823276
Woodgate Air Maintenance Ltd JAR CAA.00011 A2	018492 22789
Woodvale Hangers Ltd BCAR AMR/380 M3	017048 74497
World Aviation Support Ltd JAR CAA.00037 A1.A2.B1.B3.C1-C9.C12.C19.D1	01279 663186
World Aviation Support Ltd BCAR DAI/8864/83 A2.B3.B4 JAR CAA.00037 A1.A2.B1.B3.C1-C9.C12-C19.D1	01702 348604/348601
Wycombe Air Centre Ltd JAR CAA.00251 A2	01494 443737
Yorkshire Light Aircraft Ltd JAR CAA.00251 A1.A2.B2.C1.C3.C5.C6.C9	0113 2503133